W9-BXG-823

Document Control

Other Paton Press books by Denise Robitaille:

The Corrective Action Handbook
The Management Review Handbook
The Preventive Action Handbook
The (Almost) Painless ISO 9001:2000 Transition
Corrective Action for the Software Industry (with Johanna Rothman)
Root Cause Analysis

Document Control

A Simple Guide
to Managing Documentation

Denise Robitaille

Paton Press LLC
Chico, California

Most Paton Press books are available at quantity discounts when purchased in bulk. For more information, contact:

Paton Press LLC
P.O. Box 44
Chico, CA 95927-0044
Telephone: (530) 342-5480
Fax: (530) 342-5471
E-mail: *books@patonpress.com*
Web: *www.patonpress.com*

ISBN 1-932828-03-6

Staff
Publisher: Scott M. Paton
Managing Editor: Taran March
Book Design: David Hurst

"I get by with a little help from my friends."
–John Lennon

A brief and overdue thank you to the colleagues, clients,
and friends who have enriched my life and work.
I couldn't have done it without you.

Contents

Introduction

A few years ago I became aware of the fact that Leonardo da Vinci, one of the great Renaissance luminaries who left us such a rich legacy of art and music, inventions and scientific discovery, was also a writer of fables. The one that follows is startlingly relevant to this book on document control.

THE PAPER AND THE INK

One day, a sheet of paper was lying on a desk with other sheets just like it. It suddenly realized that it was covered with marks. A pen had written a lot of words all over it in very black ink. "Could you not have spared me this humiliation?" said the piece of paper angrily to the ink. "You have despoiled me with your horrible marks. I am ruined forever!"

"Wait!" answered the ink. "I haven't ruined you. I've covered you with words. Now you are no longer just a piece of paper, but a message. You are a guardian of man's thoughts. You have become a precious document."

Shortly thereafter someone was tidying the desk. He collected up the sheets of paper to put them on the fire. But he suddenly noticed the sheet marked by the ink. He threw the others away, but put back the one with the written message.

What a wonderful concept: a guardian of our thoughts. Part of the challenge we face when we approach the subject of document control is the question of importance. For all the rhetoric that surrounds discussions about control, access, adequacy, accuracy, and conformity, we don't spend a great deal of time talking about what documents really are.

Consider how ephemeral and illusive our great ideas would be if we didn't have this man-made device to capture them and communicate them to others. No blueprints, no chemical formulae, no signed treaties, no Declaration of Independence. Where would inventions and foundations of government be without documents?

Perhaps the sheer volume of documents we have today has dulled our sense of wonder.

Documents convey concepts over geographic boundaries and across time itself. They span continents and centuries, preserving the integrity of the authors' thoughts and conveying them to remote audiences.

The documents that are the subject of this book might not be as lofty in the messages they carry. In comparison to da Vinci's inventions, they might be quite mundane. But they're our documents. They're the guardians of our thoughts. And without them our organizations couldn't function.

Using documents is one of the ways that we perpetuate the legacy of our forefathers. We write our thoughts down so that the message can be communicated to others and preserved. It's part of our human tradition. When you consider the chaos that would result without them, you might even begin to appreciate da Vinci's perspective and think of them as "precious."

Chapter 1

What Are Documents?

D
ocuments describe requirements. They tell us what's supposed to be done and, usually, how to do it. Or they outline how things should be. For example, a bill of materials (BOM) lists what components go into a device. The technician knows that if the device isn't assembled with the components specified on the BOM, then it won't conform to defined requirements. Without the BOM, there's nothing that says what parts make up the device; the assembly requirements are undefined.

Once we begin to appreciate documents' significance to processes, we can start thinking of them in terms of what they really are: tools. Documents are one of the many resources you use to implement a process. Regardless of the nature of your organization, documents are the fundamental tools of your trade.

Documents define inputs—the grist that feeds the process mills within an organization's system. If you've got a process, then you have an input (i.e., a requirement), and that input usually is described in a document. The questions who, what, where, when, how, and why are answered in a document. We know, either directly or implicitly, who has authorized a certain action and who is authorized to perform the action. Receipt of a service call order by a field technician indicates that he or she is responsible for repairing the customer's device as directed by his or her boss, who has signed the order. The technician will do so using the schematics that were provided when he or she did the training on the retrofit for the device last month.

ISO 9001:2000 and other quality management system models place great emphasis on documents. The standard's companion guidance document, *ISO 9000:2000 Quality management systems—Fundamentals and vocabulary*, defines a document as "information and its supporting medium," and further notes that, "The medium can be paper, magnetic, electronic or optical computer disc, photograph or master sample, or a combination thereof." When considered as a whole, explains the guide, "A set of documents . . . is frequently called 'documentation.'"

The definition and supporting notes provide us with the three attributes that typify documents. They:

1. Provide information
2. Are assembled in a medium
3. Usually occur simultaneously or in conjunction with other related documents, thereby constituting a set or sets of documentation

Thus, when we speak about controlling documents, we must pay attention to their content, context, and interrelationships.

Information is the unformed clay, the essential but often unstructured raw data we need to fulfill a requirement. Documentation is the set of molds we use to form our clay into something useful.

CREATING AN INFORMED ENVIRONMENT

To be of service to an organization, documentation relies not only on *what* is said but also *how* it's said as well. The "how" isn't limited to format and also relates to such things as access, readability, timeliness, manner of communication, and method of preservation. For example, the project engineer might be responsible for generating CAD drawings for a product revision, but the information technology manager will be responsible for ensuring that access to the engineering files on the server is protected and only those who are authorized can view them. The engineer deals with the information, the manager with the electronic infrastructure in which it's contained.

There's often a third person who orchestrates the harmonization of related documents. If the newly revised product adds two steps to the manufacturing process, then someone is going to have to revise the job routers (or travelers) to include the extra tasks. Similarly, if the change is going to add seven minutes per unit to the build time, and your company makes thousands of units in a week, someone must calculate the effect on manufacturing time and then revise the production schedule accordingly. The router is the document that describes the manufacturing steps and the flow of a set of processes. The production schedule is the document that defines the sequence of job assignments in the plant and apportions the appropriate time (one of the important but often neglected resource requirements).

Other ancillary documentation such as the lead times that are maintained in an electronic document file posted on the customer service database might also need to be revised so they will continue to provide accurate information when quoting a new job. Or the equipment preventive maintenance schedule might need to be adjusted if the change means that some machinery will be used more frequently, resulting in more wear and tear on replacement parts.

BEYOND PAPER

Once we acknowledge the various and distinct attributes—i.e., content, context, and interrelationship—we can begin to understand why document control means more than just signing off on procedures. Often, context and interrelation issues are dismissed as inconsequential afterthoughts. Updating the master document list, ensuring that individuals at remote locations get copies of revisions, or checking hyperlinks on the server are too often treated like annoying details.

To fully comprehend the many aspects of document control we must think of it as a set of information about various aspects of a single subject that's formatted in different media and controlled by various and distinct functions. Understanding this basic premise is fundamental to managing the multiple interrelations of your quality management system. Just as processes are interrelated, so are the documents that define them.

There are instances when a process is so basic that a written instruction is unwarranted and wasteful. I once conducted an audit of a company that manufactured simple plastic products. They made millions each year. The packers removed the pieces that were suspended from hooks and checked them before placing them in trays. If a part wasn't acceptable, it was tossed in a scrap bin. I asked one of the packers how she knew the product was OK. She reached for her "known good" sample and, in broken English, proceeded to point out the four attributes she checked for. She grabbed a defective part and matched it up against the sample saying, "See? This one good; this one no good." The process worked perfectly. The known good sample provided all the definition that was required. In strictest terms, the sample was the document. It provided the medium within which the acceptance criteria for the product were defined.

In another part of the organization, we found documents such as:

■ Drawings
■ Chemical specification for the plastic

- Photographs
- Controlled color charts for the paint
- Production machine profiles
- Process validation parameters

This documentation formed the foundation for ensuring product conformance. Despite the fact that the packers didn't have a written instruction, there was ample supporting documentation for the process.

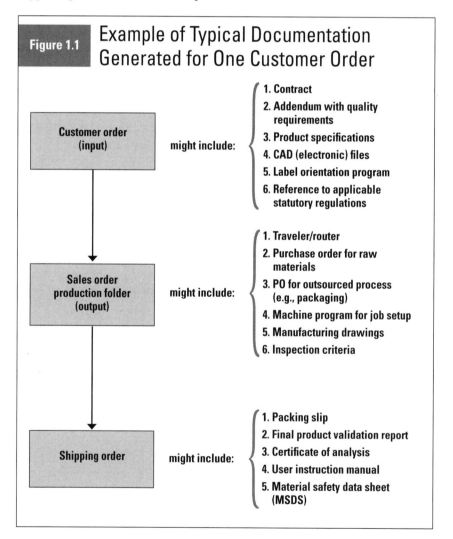

Figure 1.1   Example of Typical Documentation Generated for One Customer Order

Customer order (input) — might include:
1. Contract
2. Addendum with quality requirements
3. Product specifications
4. CAD (electronic) files
5. Label orientation program
6. Reference to applicable statutory regulations

Sales order production folder (output) — might include:
1. Traveler/router
2. Purchase order for raw materials
3. PO for outsourced process (e.g., packaging)
4. Machine program for job setup
5. Manufacturing drawings
6. Inspection criteria

Shipping order — might include:
1. Packing slip
2. Final product validation report
3. Certificate of analysis
4. User instruction manual
5. Material safety data sheet (MSDS)

INTERRELATING DOCUMENTS

Having acknowledged that sometimes you don't need a "document," the rest of this book deals with all the instances when some form of document is required.

Without a document, all you have is a good idea. An undocumented input lacks approval, definition, consensus, and consistency. No one knows who's responsible, what's supposed to be done, if there's more than one way to fulfill the requirement, and what the parameters are for determining if the activity's outcome is the desired or expected one. Often it takes more than one document to fully define, implement, and control a process.

Figure 1.1 shows a typical example of the multiple documents that can be generated for one customer order. Note that the documents represent ownership dispersed over various functions and departments, including:

■ Sales
■ Purchasing
■ Engineering
■ Manufacturing
■ Inspection
■ Shipping

The documentation includes:
■ Reference to other documents, either directly or by implication (e.g., inspection criteria might require a sampling plan)
■ Documents of external origin (e.g., customer specifications, regulatory requirements)
■ Electronic media (e.g., CAD files, machine programs)

Many of these documents in turn will link to others relating to such things as training guides, calibration requirements, and equipment maintenance schedules. They also create inputs for other processes, like the customer feedback card that you hope will be sent back after the product is installed. That in turn links to the processes for measuring customer satisfaction and can be helpful for addressing any concerns.

Figures 1.2 and 1.3 illustrate how closely the flow of documentation mirrors the flow of corresponding processes.

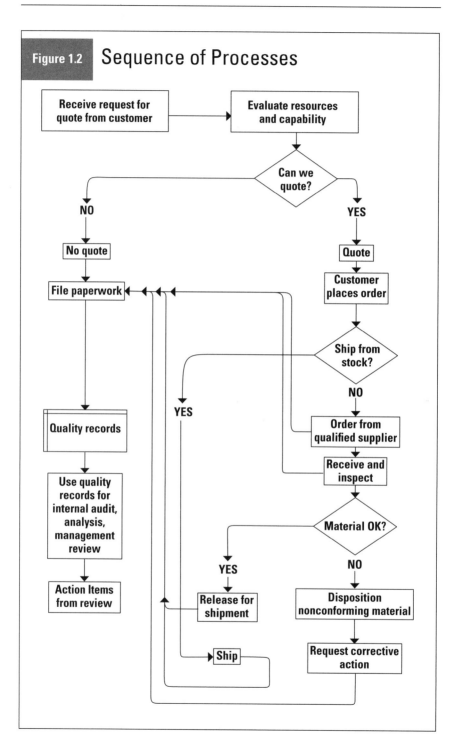

Figure 1.2   Sequence of Processes

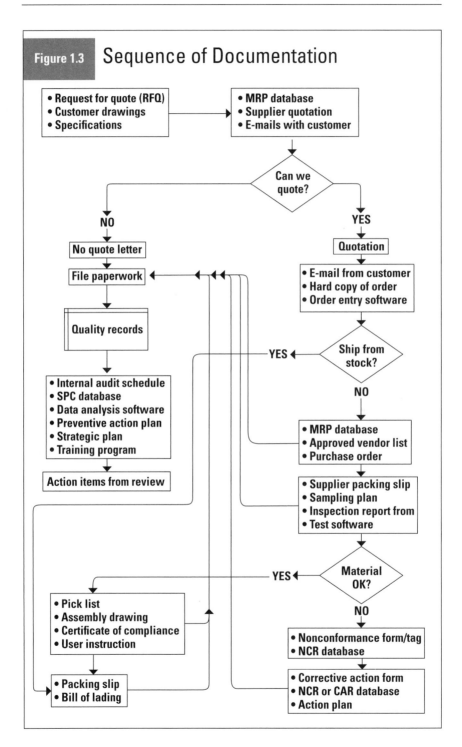

Figure 1.3 Sequence of Documentation

This book deals with various aspects of document and data control. In the next chapters we'll look at:

- Different kinds of documents
- Identifying and defining responsibility
- The relationship between documents and records
- Tips for document writers
- Managing and maintaining documents
- Issues of accessibility
- Handling revisions and deviations
- Writing document control procedures

Chapter 2

Different Kinds
of Documents

The formats and media used for defining requirements are as numerous and diverse as the processes themselves. The purpose of this chapter is to illustrate the myriad different things that come under the general heading of "documents." The nature and applicability of the conventional procedure model will be discussed along with an array of alternative formats we all use to define and control requirements. Before we can begin a discussion about generating, controlling, approving, maintaining, reviewing, and destroying documents, we must know exactly what it is that we're talking about.

Procedures have become the archetype of the quality management system (QMS) document. So ubiquitous is the use of this particular format for defining QMSs that it has inadvertently assumed the dubious distinction of being the preferred method of documenting requirements. The traditional documented procedure model follows a formulaic style with sequential, numbered sections, broken down into numbered paragraphs defining purpose, scope, responsibilities, steps, etc. For the sake of consistency and because of the pervasive use of the term "procedure" to refer to this particular style of document, this conventionally accepted definition will be used throughout this book. However, when referring to ISO 9000:2000 for a definition we find that the standard defines "procedure" as ". . . specified way to carry out an activity or a process." (Ref. 3.4.5). No mention is made of a document, let alone method of formatting.

All of this may sound oversimplified. The point is that the ISO 9001 standard doesn't require you to limit your document structure to the conventional "procedure" model. The industry practice of using this particular formatting is arbitrary and not grounded in any current mandates.

Nor is there any compelling reason to conform to the universal pyramid for organizing your documentation into three or four hierarchical tiers. It's perfectly acceptable to have, for example, procedural requirements and work instructions incorporated into one document.

Both the traditional documented procedure format and the quality documentation hierarchy are useful tools for understanding the nature and interrelation of documents, but neither of these characteristics should dominate decisions about how you organize and format your QMS requirements. Bottom line: Defining a procedure in a document is how you get a documented procedure. Don't get hung up on the minutiae of what a "documented procedure" is supposed to look like. The shape those documents take is up to you, and your time would be better spent on the content.

What ISO 9001:2000 and similar standards do require are ". . . documents needed by the organization to ensure the effective planning, operation and control of its processes . . ." (Ref. 4.2.1). The key word in this sentence is "needed." Organizations have differing degrees of complexity in their products and processes. They can employ any number of individuals and market an array of products ranging from one to several million. They have to contend with variables like education and skill levels, language barriers, regulatory requirements, workspace constraints, customer mandates, industry practices, and their own internal cultures. These factors play a significant role in determining what's "needed." The onus is on each individual organization to exercise due diligence in determining the appropriate extent and format of documents. Simple common sense should prevail.

The second important word in the ISO 9001 requirement deals with effectiveness. The following questions might help in determining if planning, operation, and control are effective. In the absence of a documented procedure, are there adequate information and control to ensure that:

■ The process owner and/or operator understand what to do?
■ The task is performed uniformly (across all shifts, for example)?
■ The output fulfills the requirements?
■ There's negligible risk of nonconformance or unacceptable variance?

If the answer to any of these questions is "no," then you probably need some kind of document.

THE PYRAMID MODEL

Before discussing the differing kinds of documents, it's appropriate to spend some time on the pyramid model that's often used to illustrate the arrangement of QMS documents (see Figure 2.1). Strict adherence to this model isn't a requirement, but it does facilitate understanding, development, and maintenance.

The pyramid demonstrates the rationale for having a framework for your documents. The quality policy expresses the organization's intent and goals. It states the organization's commitment(s). If your company were a ship, this would be the document that says where you're going. Using the same metaphor, the quality

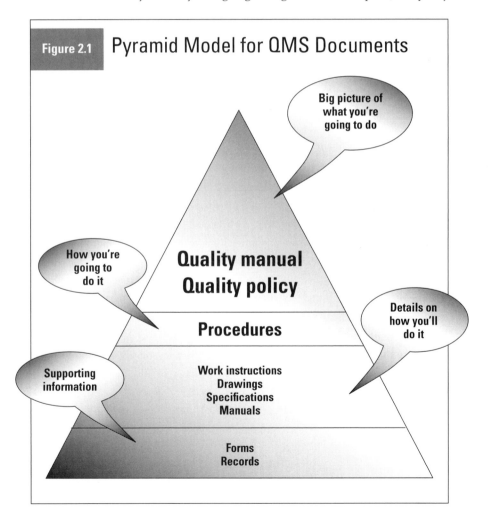

Figure 2.1 Pyramid Model for QMS Documents

manual would be your map. It describes the processes needed to fulfill the commitment made in the quality policy. It also discusses the interrelations between processes and refers to additional procedures and documents required by the organization. These descriptions generally are painted in broad strokes. The responsibility for developing both the manual and policy rests with top management.

What happens at this top level drives the documentation at all the subordinate levels. As you move down the pyramid, the documents become more specific, detailed, and compartmentalized, like the inset on a map. A documented procedure is usually well developed and provides accurate description of a process. However, it might not always extend to the details found in work instructions or drawings—documents traditionally relegated to the third tier. A procedure can create an umbrella encompassing a whole class of work instruction or tasks. For example, the procedure for controlling measuring and testing devices may reference a whole series of instructions for calibrating various instruments.

The responsibility for developing, approving, and implementing these lower tiers becomes more diffused, paralleling the organizational chart. A group leader might be responsible for writing a work instruction, a call center supervisor for generating customer-complaint handling guidelines. Encouraging authorship of lower-level documents by technicians, operators, and similar individuals increases their sense of ownership and the likelihood that the end result will accurately describe the actual practice.

Utilizing the tiers found in the pyramid model increases flexibility when dealing with revisions. One of the drawbacks of grouping instructions for multiple processes into one huge procedure means that more individuals must participate in the inevitable reviews before any revisions can be approved because more process owners are involved. This adds valueless tasks and time to an otherwise uncomplicated process. The smaller the circle of people involved, the faster the change can be approved and implemented.

Developing multiple documents for dealing with different tasks could increase the overall volume of documents. However, it dices them into manageable chunks distributed over a broader range of process owners for the purpose of review, revision, approval, communication, and retrieval. The downside is that maintaining the entire documentation system can become cumbersome and eventually uncontrolled if it isn't properly maintained.

If you use the pyramid, you end up with fewer top-level documents—the ones that provide the bird's-eye view—and more lower-level documents. These tend to increase exponentially with each descending tier. It's a neat tool to help you sort out documentation. However, there's no mandated requirement that you adhere to the model, or use it at all.

What follows are descriptions of various kinds of documents grouped by features. Although the list is comprehensive, it's not all-inclusive because many organizations have developed their own unique documentation style. Also some types of documents are industry- or sector-specific.

Occasional overlap occurs because some documents might exemplify more than one feature.

TRADITIONAL QUALITY PROCEDURES AND DOCUMENTS

This category is the conventionally accepted group of QMS documents. Because of this persisting misconception, an organization's quality function and personnel are generally presumed to have ownership of them. Unfortunately, because of the presumption, the documents get limited attention and use except during audits.

The fact that most of them are probably mandated by the QMS shouldn't diminish their value. ISO's say-so doesn't preclude the document working for you. In fact, if the document doesn't work for you, it's time to revise it or find another way of defining the corresponding requirement. The advent of ISO 9001:2000 makes it easier to migrate some of these documents away from the traditional formulaic model of numbered paragraphs to a more user-friendly and meaningful format.

In all instances, these may be in hard copy or electronic media.

Quality Manuals and Policies

This category has already been discussed. The policies relate to the organization's commitments and goals. They're generally established and developed by top management.

Quality manuals describe the organization's scope and provide an overview of the processes. The manual should not be lengthy. It shouldn't include the kind of details that are found in work instructions or other documents usually generated by process owners. ISO 9001:2000 has specific requirements for a quality manual. Subclause 4.2.2 lists the requirements as:

"a) the scope of the quality management system, including details of and justification for any exclusions,

b) the documented procedures established for the quality management system, or reference to them, and

c) a description of the interactions between the processes of the quality management system."

The reference to justifications is specifically for ISO 9001:2001 conformance. All other requirements are applicable to any quality manual, regardless of the QMS model you use. They provide an elegantly simple, concise, and clear model for articulating what you're about. The quality manual says what your company does, references documented procedures (which can be in any format you choose), and describes how processes interact. The rest of the detail is found in other documents.

Quality Procedures

These are the conventional procedures we've all become familiar with. They relate to things like inspection, purchasing, contracts, production, design, etc. Some of the titles are a holdover from ISO 9001:1994. More than any other group of documents, these tend to manifest the "scope, purpose, responsibility, and task" format with numbered paragraphs. The format has the advantages of consistency and thoroughness. If you always use the model, you're unlikely to forget to identify responsibility and authority. The structure provides prompts for document writers. It also facilitates looking things up if users know what numbered section usually deals with a particular requirement like equipment or records or forms.

There's little that's wrong with the structure, but problems can arise when the formatting itself becomes an obstacle. Some processes are better described in flowcharts; the text might be laborious and make it difficult to conceptualize an operation. Other processes are best described with a few lines of text and a lot of illustrations. And the format, like the title (i.e., procedure) is intimidating to some and suggests quality department ownership. Use this format when it works for you. Otherwise, try one of the many alternatives found in this book.

Work Instructions

This level of documents is often also referred to as SOPs, or standard operating procedures. It's at this level that the organization can exercise the greatest flexibility when deciding necessity, adequacy, formatting, and complexity. If an organization has simple processes that can be easily described, there's no reason why they can't be integrated into the quality procedures. Having an extra tier of documents may be tidy, but if it serves no purpose, it's a waste of time.

Work instructions in this category follow the same basic formatting as procedures. The two major differences are that SOPs include greater detail and tend to describe very specific tasks. As with the procedures, it's appropriate to consider alternate methods of documenting that are less conventional, such as illustrations and flowcharts.

Process sheets carry the same information as work instructions but in a less structured format. They're usually specific to one product or project.

OTHER INTERNAL DOCUMENTS

This category deals with an entire collection of documents that don't normally receive the same level of attention when establishing a documented management system. That's unfortunate. Most of these documents are already under some form of control, and they often describe requirements better than the artificial "procedures" that are generated to make auditors happy. They involve practices and formats that often predate the current QMS and have served the organization's needs effectively for years. In most cases, master copies are likely to be maintained in some form of electronic media while hard copies are distributed to relevant parties.

Travelers

These kinds of documents, also called "routers," describe the flow of a group of processes, usually in a manufacturing environment. The processes might begin with pulling raw stock or kitting components and continue through multiple operations, including in-process inspections, all the way to packaging and even shipping. Along the way, operations are signed off when complete. Travelers often reference supporting documents like drawings, bills of materials (BOMs), inspection criteria, etc. They provide traceability and communicate the status of work in progress. As controlled documents, they often provide better information than canned procedures about how a product is fabricated. When travelers are well-developed and controlled they can, in some industries, eliminate the need for production work instructions.

Drawings and Specifications

Into this category are lumped drawings, schematics, wire run charts, chemical formulae, specifications, bills of material, golden units (i.e., master samples), assembly diagrams, engineering change notices, and the like. These documents are generally considered to be within the purview of the engineering department. They're often maintained in the engineering area, accessed only by engineering staff and isolated from the rest of the organization's documentation system. When people speak of QMS documents, they rarely include CAD files or blueprints in the conversation.

This practice can create artificial barriers and contribute to the breakdown between processes, perpetuating the problematic perception that quality procedures are owned by the quality manager, and other documents are owned by other functions. Everyone must recognize that all documents are part of the system. While it's appropriate, and probably more efficient, to have process owners retain responsibility for documents relating to their functions, it's important to establish adequate communication and access to ensure that required interfaces and reviews occur.

ISO 9001:2000 doesn't require a "documented procedure" for design control. It does require organizations to: ". . . plan and control the design and development of the product." It's perfectly acceptable to use, for example, Gantt charts to establish timelines, milestones, planned reviews, and necessary interfaces for a design project. These, along with product specifications, requirements, failure modes and effects analysis (FMEA), and similar inputs are the documents that define your process. The thoroughness of this documentation, level of control, accessibility, consistent adherence to plans, and relevance to other processes in the organization determines if your design process is adequately defined and documented. The upside is that you don't need a wordy "procedure" that creates little value for the engineers. The downside is that engineering must treat these documents as part of the QMS and recognize the need for appropriate interfaces, including considerations for access.

This is the first category that includes documents of external origin. Drawings and specifications, regardless of the medium, can originate with the customer. This introduces the additional criterion of ownership. Unlike all the documents mentioned so far, these are owned by an external entity. Maintaining documents of external origin is discussed later in the chapter.

Finally, just as with travelers, the information on a drawing or an assembly diagram could be adequate enough to eliminate the need for a wordy written procedure.

Schedules

Schedules are documents that say when things must happen. Most organizations typically have schedules for the following:

- Production
- Internal quality audits
- Calibration
- Equipment maintenance
- Refresher training

It's unnecessary to have a procedure detailing what the schedule is, then an actual schedule, and finally a form to fill out demonstrating that the task has been completed in accordance with the schedule and/or procedure. A document can be formatted to accommodate the definition and communication of the requirements on the same page where the sign-off for completion is recorded. Upside: no wordy procedure; downside: must be controlled because it's a document.

Contracts

Contracts can come in many forms, although the ones most often dealt with in a typical QMS are customer orders and the purchase orders you place with your vendors. Others can include service agreements, letters of intent, memoranda of understanding, and actual contracts. In all instances they are documents that define a customer's requirements as communicated to a supplier. Like other documents, they create the input to successive processes. Customer purchase orders are the input to the manufacturing and/or purchasing process; purchase orders define the inputs for the incoming receiving process. They can, and often do, define product requirements that exceed the scope of design specifications. For example, they might include packaging, labeling, delivery, or validation requirements. Contracts can define the deliverables from an outsourced process, such as off-site records archiving. Fulfilling the requirement is the output of the process, as defined in the contract.

Unlike most documents discussed so far, contracts either originate from outside the organization or generate an input that must be fulfilled from outside. They embody the communication of requirements between two stakeholders in different organizations and create an effective interface between two separate QMSs. Regardless of the format or the point of origin, contracts define requirements that must be met to serve the customer. This amplifies the need to ensure that the requirements are understood and agreed upon, so that the contract can be fulfilled.

The manner in which contracts are controlled is covered later in this and subsequent chapters.

Strategic Plans

These are the documents that define the organization's goals, usually in terms of budgetary allocations, capital expenditures, new market ventures, and similar high-level decisions. Like the quality policy and quality manual, they drive the requirements at subordinate layers of the organization. Budgets are the monetary articulation of resource allocation as identified through activities such as management review, results of internal training assessment needs, audits, and new design projects. Capital expenditures relate to issues such as production capacity and improved telecommunication technologies. New market ventures drive the requirements for design projects.

These documents are often omitted from QMS documentation because they're considered proprietary. Unfortunately, they're also excluded because of the persisting perception that there are QMS documents, and then there are the "real" documents for running the company. A simple mention in your document control procedure of these documents will go far toward recognizing that quality and business requirements are the same thing.

Job Descriptions and Training Guides

These two categories are grouped together because they define the requirements relating to the organization's human resource. Job descriptions provide the basic specifications for a particular position or task. For example, to be hired as a software engineer, an applicant might need to demonstrate proficiency with certain operating systems, computer languages, and programs. She or he must have worked a certain number of years in a comparable environment. Those are the minimum requirements to be qualified or deemed competent to perform the job.

You can't determine if someone is qualified for a task if you haven't defined what the requirements are for qualification. Nor can you assess training needs if you haven't defined what you need people to be able to do.

Training guides are the tools you use to help people achieve qualification or competency. They're the output of an assessment of training needs. When developed into an instructional format, these documents help individuals attain a level of competency or qualification to perform certain tasks. Like many other QMS requirements, they're dynamic and subject to change when new products are introduced, technologies improve, staff gets promoted, or additional equipment is acquired.

Job descriptions and training guides are documents that create a set of specifications for fulfilling the organization's human resource requirements.

User Manuals and Product Literature

These two groups of documents relate to customer requirements. Product literature defines features of the product and, in some cases, creates an implicit contract that the product, with specifications as published, is what will be furnished in the event of an order. User manuals are a part of the product deliverables, especially if the product can't be used without them.

The reason these documents are grouped together is because they're often generated outside of the organization, as an outsourced process. Graphic designers, technical writers, printers, and even mail-handling services all have a part in creating and delivering these kinds of documents. Again, because they're not in a conventional document format, they're often discounted as QMS documents. And because they're products of outsourced processes, the essential interfaces with appropriate functions within the organization are overlooked, leading to inconsistencies and miscommunications: The product gets revised, for example, but the assembly instructions remain the same as in the older version.

Unconventional Documents and Formats

Bearing in mind that the definition of a document doesn't limit the media in which the information is contained, there are additional effective and reliable methods for communicating and controlling requirements.

White boards can be used for posting the schedule for the day—or the week. I've seen them used to communicate the status of work in process and to flag problems or rush jobs. They define part of the planning process in a way that's understood by the production staff. Appropriately monitored and controlled, this is an elegantly simple document.

Posters and other posted notices can also serve as documents. Sometimes they're derived from procedures and put into a format that's easy for everyone to read without having to open a binder or access an electronic file. Other times they're stand-alone requirements formatted for maximum visibility.

Known good samples, also called "golden units," are perhaps the most unconventional documents. With these, the requirements are defined by the object. The tacit message is: "If you build the device so that it's just like this one, it will meet the required specifications." The biggest challenge with golden units is ensuring that they're revised when the corresponding documents (e.g., drawings, schematics, etc.) are revised.

DOCUMENTS OF EXTERNAL ORIGIN

This section deals with documents that aren't created by the organization but that define requirements necessary for fulfilling customer expectations. Unlike those generated internally, it's not possible to approve or revise these documents. The authority for revisions exists with the originator.

The typical problem that arises with this category is that, because documents of external origin aren't created by the organization, individuals don't perceive them as part of the QMS documentation. Organizations that use them must ensure that personnel understand their responsibilities vis-à-vis these documents' maintenance and disposition.

The control exercised over these documents relates to:

- Access
- Preservation
- Awareness of the status of revisions
- Information on how to obtain the most current revision
- Harmonizing requirements from external documents with requirements of internally generated documents.

What follows are brief descriptions of the most typical documents of external origin used.

National and/or International Standards

If you are registered to ISO 9001:2000 or a similar QMS, the standard that defines the requirements of your QMS is one of your documents of external origin. Defining where it's kept and facilitating appropriate access is one of the ways you ensure that the quality manager isn't the only person who knows what it says.

Customer Specifications

Customer drawings are the most common form of specifications. Others include contracts, orders, quality requirements, packaging, labeling and shipping information, and inspection and/or test reporting requirements. They can come attached to purchase orders or as separate booklets and binders. The can be hard copy, samples, or electronic media such as CAD drawings or Gerber files.

Specifications require additional precautions because they often contain proprietary data and intellectual property. Customers, in some instances, even define the retention period and method of disposal for the documents they send you.

Statutory and Regulatory Requirements

These documents define requirements or laws imposed upon your organization by governmental agencies. They may relate to your product, facility, employees, or one of your processes. Product release criteria can be regulated by agencies like the Food and Drug Administration for medical devices and pharmaceuticals. Those criteria are defined in 21 CFR Part 820 published in the Federal Register of the

Department of Health and Human Services. The Occupational Safety and Health Administration (OSHA) has responsibility for the health and safety requirements relating to work environments, equipment, and personnel. If you have a chemical process that results in the need to treat wastewater, the requirements for part of the process are probably defined in an environmental regulation. Failure to comply with any of these statutes can result in fines, legal action, or shutdown, which would definitely affect your ability to serve your customers.

ISO 9001:2000 specifically requires organizations to determine if there are any ". . . statutory and regulatory requirements related to the product . . ." (Ref: 7.2.1). If you are in a regulated industry, your process owners (engineers, for example) must have access to the documents that define statutory product requirements.

Industry and Product Standards

Into this group you can put any of the requirements that are specific to your industry. They're very similar to regulatory requirements and include generally accepted guidelines and directives reached by industry consensus, managed by recognized bodies, and handed down through associations, professional societies, and similar entities. Some typical examples include the IPC standard (Association Connecting Electronic Industries) for acceptability of electronic assemblies, military specifications, UL or CE product marking, or any of the hundreds of standards promulgated and managed by organizations such as the Institute of Electrical and Electronic Engineers (IEEE), American National Standards Institute (ANSI), and the National Electrical Manufacturers Association (NEMA), to name just a few.

Operating and Repair Manuals

This last group is small and often forgotten. The importance of these documents depends on the criticality and complexity of the equipment. Controlling these documents is probably just a matter of ensuring that key people know where they are. It's not uncommon to find them filed in a locked cabinet where only one person (who occasionally goes on vacation) stores them for safekeeping.

ELECTRONIC MEDIA

To fully understand the requirements for handling electronic documentation, we must remember the ISO 9000:2000 definition: "information and its supporting medium." Sometimes software issues deal with information; at other times, they deal with the medium. It's not always easy to distinguish the two. Computer-aided design (or CAD) files contain data; CAD programs provide the structure within which data can be displayed and manipulated in an intelligible format. It gets more complicated when you also consider the platform or operating system, i.e., the software that allows different programs to interact and function in the virtual architecture that has been developed. The reliability of all of these ultimately is founded on the integrity of the computer, server, and/or network.

In the software industry the product being furnished can be the actual software program, a device into which the software is embedded, or a product reliant on interfaces with devices and/or software designed and sold by other businesses. Tracking the various versions and revisions of software is critical. Configuration management is the conventional methodology for handling the control of these virtual documents and for ensuring the reliability of information relating to status and traceability.

For these reasons we must ensure adequate control of electronic media. Unfortunately, because databases and electronic files aren't always perceived as documentation, they don't get defined as such in QMS documents. The fact that responsibility for maintenance might lie with the information management system manager doesn't diminish the need to ensure these documents' proper integration into the organization's documentation. The information must be managed so that it facilitates the link to the QMS requirements they define.

The chart in Figure 2.2 illustrates the relationship between some electronic media and the corresponding processes in the QMS. It demonstrates how reliant we've become on this form of documentation and how critical it is that we approach it with a comparable level of attention to definition and control.

Thus, when you're dealing with different kinds of documents, your options for defining and controlling a QMS are abundant and richly varied. They provide you with a broad enough selection to choose a format and style that's most appropriate for your organization.

| Figure 2.2 | Electronic Media and QMS Requirements | |

Electronic Media	Related QMS Requirements	Relevant ISO 9001:2000 Clauses
Test software	– Design validation – Process validation – Product acceptance/release – Control of measuring devices	7.3.1, 7.3.5, 7.3.6, 7.4.3, 7.6, 8.2.4, 8.3
ERP database	– Managing inventory (e.g., traceability, lot control, shelf life) – Linkage to customer product requirements – Planning/ability to fulfill requirements in a timely manner	7.2.1, 7.4.1, 7.4.2, 7.5.1, 7.5.3, 7.5.4, 7.5.5
CAD files	– Product specifications (including customer-owned requirements) – Design specifications – All other product- and design-related software (e.g., Gerber files)	7.2.1, 7.3.2, 7.5.1, 7.5.4
Data management programs and software	– Programs for handling documents (including electronic signature approvals) – Databases for collecting, processing, and analyzing performance metrics for various QMS processes (e.g., supplier on-time delivery, production scrap) – Bar-coding, job-tracking database – Linking of defects database with nonconformance and corrective action databases – Any program that facilitates interface between functions	4.2.3, 4.2.4, 7.5.3, 8.2.2, 8.3, 8.4, 8.5.2, 8.5.3
CNC programs	– Define/control machining processes	7.5.2, 8.2.3
Web site	– Communicate product offerings, specifications, and capabilities to customers – E-commerce	5.2, 7.2.1, 7.2.3
Intranet/e-mail	– Internal communication – Communication with customers and vendors – Records of approvals, authorizations, concessions, change orders, and other pertinent information – Media for self-directed learning/ training	4.2.3, 5.5.3, 6.2.2, 7.2.2, 7.2.3, 7.4.2, 8.2.4, 8.3

Chapter 3

Identifying Owners and Defining Responsibility

Your documentation system, just like your entire quality management system (QMS), is the responsibility of many people. There are numerous players with varying degrees of accountability. The number of individuals involved in document control depends on the size of your organization and the complexity of your processes—again, just like everything else.

The interrelation of your documents should mirror the interrelation of your processes. Therefore, the persons working at the junction of those interrelations must communicate with one another. For example, if there's a relationship between product design and development of user manuals, the individuals who have responsibility for each set of documents must be in communication, and the resulting documentation should reflect that communication and the interaction's effectiveness.

Responsibility for documents is shared. If a procedure or work instruction is going to be useful, the manner in which it's written and formatted must be comprehensible to the operator or technician. The documents' users have a reciprocal responsibility to let authors and document managers know if the instructions are ambiguous or downright wrong.

Responsibility for various aspects of document control can run the gamut from authoring, approving, revising, maintaining, and disposal to simply using. It's important to recognize and articulate each of those responsibilities.

In a small company you have fewer people wearing more hats; in a larger enterprise sometimes several people are assigned to do the same kind of tasks. Therefore, the categories that follow represent tasks rather than persons. In all cases, it's important to remember that, with the exception of very large organizations, these activities are just part of the many assignments that make up one person's job.

AUTHORS

These are the individuals who are responsible for creating the documents. In the typical QMS, the job of developing the organization's procedures falls to the quality assurance manager. However, there are, as we've seen, a whole universe of other documents that organizations use every day. The authors of those other documents (e.g., drawings, specifications, schedules, formulae, flowcharts, databases, etc.) must be held to the same level of accountability for the relevance and clarity of their documents. That can't happen, if "procedures" are the only documents covered in a company's document control process. All relevant documents must be included, regardless of format or origin.

Most readers of this book will already have some documents in place. Once the considerable mass of information is integrated into the documentation infrastructure, it's possible to review whether that information is written in a useful and effective format. Going forward this affords you the potential to establish guidelines that will result in documents that are more appropriately and consistently linked, mitigating incidents of ambiguity and conflicting data.

Authors must consider their audience. The purpose of a document is not only to define a requirement but also to communicate it to the process owner. Regardless of the format, persons generating documentation should be conscious of their readers. If the intended user can't understand the requirement as defined, it's of little value. Included in this list of authors are those individuals who generate electronic media such as forms, software programs, databases, and the like. They're as accountable as the authors of procedures and other written requirements, so make sure that the information is comprehensible to the intended user.

Organizations should encourage process owners to take more active roles in the authorship of the work instructions and procedures that define their processes.

DOCUMENT COORDINATORS

In larger organizations, the position of document coordinator is used to manage the documentation infrastructure. If documents are retained electronically, the coordinator creates the necessary interface between the information management system department and the various process owners. These individuals often are tasked with ensuring the harmonization and interrelation of documents from different departments and functions. Also, they typically develop and manage document packets for complex products with multiple components, assemblies, and subassemblies. They make sure required documents are included and the packet is complete. This is all good news.

The only problem that sometimes arises is when the document coordinator's role expands to include the actual interface between process owners—the reviews and interactions that usually result in authorizations and approvals. Rather than simply being responsible for managing the document systems (i.e., the output of the interactions between interrelated processes), the individual ends up functioning like a reviewer, assuming inappropriate ownership for the content as well as the context.

CUSTODIANS AND LIBRARIANS

These individuals are responsible for making sure that documents are stored and preserved. Their role is similar to that of document coordinators, except it's usually limited to storage. This might include archiving older documents that need to be retained for regulatory or contractual reasons. Remember that the categories listed here reflect functions rather than job descriptions, so this activity is rarely a stand-alone job. A typical example would be the administrative support person in the engineering department who has—among other tasks—responsibility for cataloging and preserving blueprints.

Effectively fulfilling this custodial part of the process helps to ensure appropriate access, ease of retrieval, smooth transition of revisions, and proper handling of obsolete documents.

REVISER, EDITORS, REVIEWERS, APPROVERS

Once a document has been created, it can go through multiple revisions and changes during its lifetime. It's not uncommon for controversy to arise about who's responsible for managing the revisions. A typical scenario might involve changes to the manufacturing documents for a product. The engineering department has ownership of prerelease documents, but ownership transfers to the product manager once the product becomes a regular catalog offering. Any document revisions resulting from minor modifications get lost in a quagmire of snarled miscommunications.

To ensure against documentation system breakdowns, when a part or process is revised it's essential to ensure that responsibility for various activities is defined. Questions to ask include:

- Who's responsible for initiating the change?
- Who assesses ancillary documentation to ensure continued compatibility and consistency?
- Who's authorized to approve an initial document and/or a revision? Do you need more than one signatory?
- Are there statutory constraints on revision control? Do you need to notify or seek approval from a regulatory body? If so, who does it?
- What role do the reviewers play? Are these individuals different from the approvers? And if so, how do they communicate their input to those who manage the revisions?
- If several departments and/or functions must review the revisions, how are those interfaces and transitions handled? Who manages the "traffic" along the path of process owners?

USERS

Often people who use documents are treated like passive receptors, even though it's for their benefit that the documents exist. If it wasn't necessary to define a requirement for the purpose of communicating it to another individual, then creating and maintaining documents would be an esoteric exercise at best. At worst, it becomes a meaningless consumption of precious resources.

The users may be internal or external. Brochures, manuals, and Web sites all provide information for users who are external to the organization. Targeting the format and content so that it's useful—and appealing—to them is part of your relationship with your customers. The formatting, language, and content must be comprehensible to them. This is another of the myriad interrelations in your QMS.

Instructions, procedures, drawings, and other specifications are the tools for communicating requirements to your internal customers. Unlike the external users, internal customers have shared ownership of documentation. Part of their responsibility is to inform their supervisors or the appropriate process owner about factual errors or if the instructions don't appear to make sense. Often, audits reveal that documents don't reflect actual practice. The process owner ends up getting blamed for a nonconformance instead of being recognized for ignoring a procedure that was obviously wrong. The problem could lie with a practice that discourages process owners from communicating with authors and that perpetuates the misconception that quality people are automatically the best authors of documents. The outcome is documentation that might have a very pretty format but that's neither complete nor correct.

Organizations fail to let operators know that they can play an active part in creating and revising documents. Technicians, operators, line workers, sales personnel, and the like should be encouraged to share ideas and communicate problems. They need to know their input is valuable. They must share ownership for the documents' contents.

Users need to:

- Provide input into documents that describe their processes
- Know whom to talk to if a document is wrong or a process has changed
- Know how to care for documents
- Have appropriate access to documents
- Be able to recognize the approval status and revision level (when appropriate) of documents

OUTSOURCING

Any outsourced process that includes developing documentation must include consideration for how the documents are generated. Typical examples include:

- Drawings and specifications from a design firm
- All the output from the developers of manuals and brochures
- Test validation protocols from an independent lab
- Customer complaint database from an outsourced call center

Providers of outsourced processes should be qualified in accordance with the organization's defined procedures (often as part of the purchasing function), and the appropriate interfaces with the internal process owner should be adequately defined. This ensures the compatibility of requirements and diminishes incidents of conflicting information.

COMMUNICATORS, DISTRIBUTORS, TRAINERS, FACILITATORS

"The devil is in the details." So says an anonymous German proverb. This final category includes all the often-unnamed souls who have responsibility for activities that are regularly forgotten—or that someone assumes another person will handle. Failure to address the details related to this last category has caused many a documentation snafu.

"Communicators" is a simple catchall heading for all the people whose joint responsibility it is to say:

- "The document has been revised."
- "There's a new procedure."
- "Here's where you can go to find the new version of that specification."
- "The schedule has changed."
- "We aren't using that form anymore."

. . . and any other communication relating to documents.

Communications can be verbal, sent by e-mail, stapled to the new procedure when it's distributed, or part of a formal notification process. The important thing to remember is that someone has to handle this detail.

Distributors handle getting the new documents to the users and retrieving the obsolete copies when there's a revision. Distribution is sometimes facilitated by using a matrix that defines who has hard copy of documents or who has access. Distribution can be electronic, which would entail removing obsolete versions from general access and putting the new documents out on the server. Notification is sometimes included in this activity.

Trainers come into the picture when a new or revised document requires employees to receive instruction or refresher training. If you want process owners to really use the documents, you can emphasize their importance by ensuring that everyone knows and understands what changed from the last version. Passing out documents and blithely assuming that everyone will get the variation is another one of those "devil in the details" scenarios waiting for an opportunity to happen.

"Facilitators" is a wrap-up category that covers everyone who's willing to pitch in and make sure the changes are implemented, communicated, and understood—and that nothing gets forgotten.

Documentation doesn't exist for its own sake. It's created by one entity to communicate to another the defined requirements of a third party for the purpose of satisfying requirements generated by one or several other groups of people. In a well-integrated QMS, documentation can become a very intricate network. But without people, documents are just paper and ink and bytes of data piling up on desks and hard drives.

Chapter 4

The Relationship Between Documents and Records

There's a direct correlation between documents and records. Documents provide the definition of requirements. Records furnish evidence of fulfilling those requirements. Documents relate to inputs; records relate to outputs. Together they manifest the purest example of the concept of "process." (See Figure 4.1)

A series of inputs and outputs creates a chain of processes, as illustrated in Figures 4.2 and 4.3. Outputs from one process become inputs to the next. Similarly, the record of fulfillment for one process authorizes the initiation of the next. The record of fulfilling the purchasing function, for example, is a requisition that embodies the definition of the inputs for the next process (i.e., the acceptance requirements for incoming inspection).

ISO 9000:2000 defines a process as a ". . . set of interrelated or interacting activities which transform input into outputs." (Ref 3.4.1)

Documents and records are intimately linked. You can't generate a record if you don't have an output—the outcome of a process. You can't have an outcome if you didn't do anything. You can't do anything if you don't know what you're

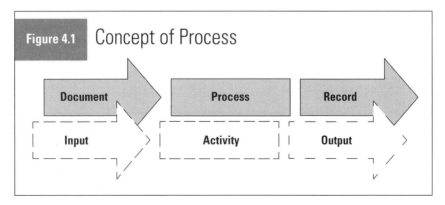

Figure 4.1 Concept of Process

Document → Process → Record

Input > Activity > Output >

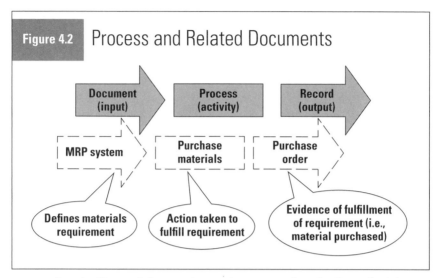

Figure 4.2   Process and Related Documents

supposed to do. You can't know what you're supposed to do if you don't have a requirement—the input to your process. Thus, it's impossible to generate a record if you don't have a requirement to match it up against. The conventional method of defining requirements is with a document.

Just as organizations must decide what documents they need, they also must assess what records are required. If a record's intent is to demonstrate and communicate the outcome of a process and the fulfillment of a requirement, it's possible for that evidence to be something other than a piece of paper or an electronic record. The quality management system (QMS) requires the process to be controlled. A simple example of evidence is using bins to define product status. Line workers who check hundreds of widgets every day shouldn't be expected to generate records for each article. Oftentimes, placement is used to denote the outcome of an inspection: Pieces in the red bin are scrap; those in the blue bin are OK to send on to packaging. With these situations, you must ask, "In the absence of a written (or electronic) record, is there:

■ Adequate evidence that the outcome of the process is what was required?
■ Enough information to permit the initiation of the next process?
■ Appropriate control to ensure the results are known and acceptable?"

This chapter deals with those instances when the answer is "no." The premise is that a written or electronic record has been created.

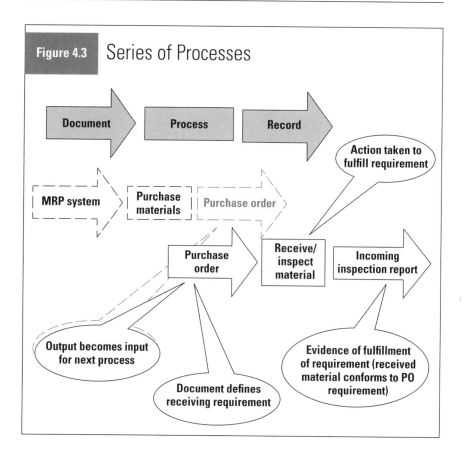

Figure 4.3 Series of Processes

EVIDENCE OF COMPLIANCE

There are sector-specific and statutory constraints on record keeping that are unique to certain industries. For example, the medical device industry is required to maintain extensive device history records. Organizations are required to comply with the record-retention mandates of their customers and regulatory bodies. Additionally, there are quality records specifically required by ISO 9001:2000 and other QMS models.

Your documentation should provide either implicit or explicit criteria to determine if the requirements, as defined in a document, have been fulfilled. To effectively verify the result, it's important to assess how adequately the requirement has been defined. If the outcome isn't what was expected, there are several possible reasons, all tied to the definition of requirements:

- The requirement wasn't correctly described.
- The requirement wasn't adequately defined.
- The method or process to fulfill the requirement wasn't adequate or appropriately defined.
- The criteria for determining fulfillment weren't adequately defined.
- The methodology for verification wasn't adequately defined.

EVIDENCE OF PROCESS CONTROL

Records do more than just tell you if a product or process succeeded. Records can help you determine how well you're controlling the processes you use to serve your customers. If your definitions and controls are inadequate, the fallout could far exceed the occasional product defect. Your organization might begin to experience breakdowns relating to several factors, all traceable to document control. Because the process approach is so fundamental to ISO 9001:2000 and similar QMS models, it's important for process owners to comprehend the distinction between documents and records. The distinction corresponds directly to the relationship between process inputs and outputs.

A valuable exercise is to select representative documents and see if people can identify the corresponding records or other evidence of fulfillment. The illustration in Figure 4.4 is an example of how that might look. When the chart is complete you'll have a fair representation of your documented requirements and the kind of records you keep. This chart can also be used to facilitate the development of audit plans and checklists.

CLARIFYING THE QMS

Documents and records also help stakeholders understand the quality system. Process owners can better conceptualize the idea of internal customers and recognize their roles as the customers of inputs (i.e., defined requirements) and the suppliers of outputs (i.e., records of fulfillment). Finally, well-developed documents and reliable records can help you effectively implement other processes such as internal auditing, preventive action, risk management, root cause analysis, and corrective action.

Figure 4.4	Document/Corresponding Record Chart

Document	Requirement	Record	Alternate Evidence of Fulfillment
Dwg. 78334 Rev. B	– Bore diameter 0.749 +/- 0.005	– Inspection record form	
	– Length 3.25 +/- .01	– (Same)	
	– 303 stainless	– Certificate of analysis	
Production schedule	– Shipping date to customer	– Invoice in accounting	
Procedure P44-16	– Review of design requirements	– Electronic project tracking software	
	– Authorization to proceed with BETA phase	– Signature of VP on final design report	
	– Authorize design of product literature		Product literature
Procedure P48-21	– Order entry		Order in database
	– Review for completeness; ability to meet delivery date	– Stamp with initials on hard copy of customer order	
Procedure P49-05	– Quarterly pest control	– Invoice from service provider	
Job order 78943 Rev. A and router (same no.) (Router bar-coded; corresponds to tracking software)	– Machine	– Job tracking database	
	– De-burr	– (Same)	
	– Heat treat (outsourced)	– Final test report from vendor	
	– Individually package	– Job tracking database	
Customer additional specifications	– Protection of intellectual property/proprietary data		– Secure files on server; password protected
Procedure P49-01	– Identify nonconforming material	– Large hold tag with identification and disposition	
	– Segregate defective product		– Locked cabinet
	– Get concession from customer	– E-mail files	

A peculiar characteristic of documents is that they sometimes become records. An open contract or purchase order defines the requirements from the customer or to a supplier. They authorize action. However, once they're complete, they become records of the fulfillment of the requirement. If you use a form to record equipment preventive maintenance, and it includes such PM requirements as grease fittings, change filters, check oil level, etc., then the form is the document that describes the process. When it's filled out, it becomes the record of fulfillment.

When asked to describe the difference between documents and records, I draw the following analogy. Documents are living; records are dead. A document is a dynamic instrument that you use to know what to do and how to do it. It grants permission, provides guidance, and communicates deliverables. It can be revised. A record is an inert terminal that preserves evidence that the requirements of a document have been fulfilled. A record can be appended (i.e., added to), but it can't be revised—unless you're committing fraud.

Chapter 5

Tips for
Document Writers

The single most important rule when generating documents is to consider your audience. Who are going to use the documents? Although it's irrefutable that documentation content must be accurate, if the requirements themselves are incomprehensible, they're worthless. Remember that documents are tools. They must be useful to the persons who have to refer to them.

Standardize and simplify. Use a standard format. If you have different kinds of documents, settle on a select few styles and formats. Ensure that a consensus exists among people generating documents. Conduct training if necessary.

The standard "procedure" format is optimum for certain kinds of documents—usually those found on the conventional pyramid model's second tier and that describe requirements thoroughly but without elaborate details. Procedures have a predictable appearance, and people are often familiar with them. Use this format for any process that will benefit from that formal structure. Make sure people understand the meaning and function of headings. Some of them, notably purpose and scope, often are written with little attention to what they actually say.

- *Purpose:* Tells why someone would reference this document. Individuals should be able to read the purpose and know whether they have their hands on the right document. For example, "The purpose of this document is to describe how applications for loans are processed at branch locations."

- *Scope:* This focuses on content. Readers should be able to tell at a glance what particular activities are included. For example, "The scope of this procedure is to describe the various forms that are required for consumer loan applications, information that must be communicated to the applicant, collection and input of consumer information from applications, process for review, and the report that is generated." Note that the scope here doesn't include approval or notification to the applicant of the outcome of the review. The scope is limited to very specific activities.

If care is consistently given to the text found in these kinds of headers, the information should diminish the time process owners spend trying to find the right document.

Most authors of procedures use a conventional, numbered procedure format. If you do, it's often beneficial to assign pre-established categories to the sections. For example:

1. Purpose
2. Scope
3. Equipment
4. Responsibility
5. Process
6. Labeling, identification, status
7. Related documents
8. Records
9. History of revisions

Categories can be combined. For example: purpose and scope, or documents and records. Should the process not require any particular equipment, the category is simply marked "N/A." Thus, even if one or two categories get skipped, records will always be found in section eight. Consistency is the aim.

Establish comparable guidelines for other document styles. In all instances they should be concise and uncomplicated. They can relate to structure, placement of revision-level information, location of approvals signatures, and other document control requirements. These facilitate users' ability to determine if they have the right document and an approved version.

Limit the number of verbose procedures. Choose simpler formats whenever it's possible and appropriate. Different formats can include any of the following.

BULLETED LIST

This is simply a list of steps to follow. It can include check boxes or space for sign-offs. These can serve as the record for completing a task or simply as a tickler so that individuals don't forget important steps. Bulleted lists can also be posted on a wall. Instructions that are made into posters are very effective documents, as long as they're controlled. Control can be as simple as having an authorized signature and assessing the information's continued applicability during an audit or document/process revision.

ILLUSTRATIONS

It's said that a picture is worth a thousand words. Work environments populated by individuals from around the globe often face the challenge of language barriers. In some organizations, the educational level of the staff is varied and often not very advanced. And then, some things are just better understood in a picture format, regardless of the number of university degrees you have hanging on the wall. Improvements in digital photography, coupled with the increasing affordability of the technology, make the utilization of photos, pictures, and illustrations more commonly acceptable, practical, and effective. Use them solely or in conjunction with simple documents.

FORMS

A well-developed form with the appropriate information about a process is an efficient technique for documenting requirements. It carries the additional benefit of incorporating the record of fulfillment.

Design forms that work for you. Avoid the temptation to acquire (borrow, buy, benchmark) a "canned" form from outside of the organization, unless you commit to modifying it before use. Companies often try to save time by using a format that they've seen used elsewhere. There are plenty of templates for sale in the quality marketplace. Some of them are creatively laid out and filled with great ideas. They can be useful for companies that are just starting out. Problems arise when organizations try to use the forms without adapting them adequately to their own processes and documentation structure. They end up with forms that have spaces which make no sense, and so the information is only half filled out. Or the form is used incorrectly because the language, acronyms, or style are alien to the people who are expected to use them.

If forms are to be used as documents, they need to be controlled, and there must be consensus (and/or training) as to their use.

FLOWCHARTS

The promulgation of the process approach to define and implement quality management systems (QMSS) has dramatically increased the use of flowcharts to define processes. They're wonderful tools for illustrating the inputs and outputs of a series of processes and are remarkably useful in analyzing constraints and breakdowns.

Flowcharts can be extremely sophisticated, employing an array of shapes to denote process, decision point, database, records, etc. However, not everyone has equal familiarity with this format. It bears repeating: Remember to consider your audience. Before embarking on a project to flowchart all of your processes, ensure that people understand the technology or budget for the necessary training so that they will. Make sure the application is consistent among all the flowchart authors or developers.

Just as with illustrations, flowcharts can be stand-alone documents or incorporated into work instructions and similar documents.

MEMOS

If you use memos to communicate requirements, you have to exercise appropriate control over them. They're an inexpensive and usually effective method of conveying important information. The most practical way to achieve control is by having consistent practices as to the use, approval, and distribution of memos. Decide what kind of memos must be controlled, and choose a format that's used exclusively for these communications. Some companies refer to them as "alerts." They should state the subject matter, the requirement, the date, and the approval. Strive to develop a format that's visually unique. Print them on different-colored paper to differentiate them from other memos and to make them more noticeable.

ELECTRONIC FORMS AND DATABASES

Information management system personnel have a unique challenge when creating documents for internal users. The information they generate is written in binary code, a language that's foreign to most laypeople. Defining the requirements for QMS document applications is no less arduous a task than developing specifications for a software product. Also, as we've mentioned, with software applications the line between the information and the medium is often blurred. An electronic form not only communicates data but also inherently encompasses the information for linking that data to other information. Developers of these kinds of forms, as well as databases for gathering and analyzing data and programs to link all the information, must understand what it is that the users wish to accomplish.

Users, for their part, must understand that they have to be literal and thorough in describing their requirements. Software people can't write the electronic documents that are needed if they don't fully comprehend the purpose of the requirement. Assumptions as to intent and requirements are a common stumbling block. Create templates to define specifications. Conduct meetings; invite facilitators to help out. Make sure that all parties agree as to content, context, access, and necessary interfaces.

GENERAL GUIDELINES

What follows are some general guidelines that are applicable to all documentation, regardless of the media.

Pay attention to the language that you use. Avoid flowery and overly clever vocabulary. Make sentences short. Avoid ambiguity. Get to the point.

People in some industries speak in a veritable alphabet soup, using acronyms for forms, processes, instruments, and products. Sometimes it's a more efficient way of communicating. Limit the use of acronyms and abbreviations, unless you're confident everyone knows what they mean. If you have to use them, develop a reference glossary to make sure there is consensus on what they mean and to help out new hires, temps, and outside contractors.

Avoid saying things twice. Whenever you describe the same process in more than one document, you increase the risk of creating instructions with conflicting information. It makes control of revisions a nightmare. Rather, refer to related documents. For example, when describing the process for addressing customer complaints, make reference to the procedure for handling nonconformances. The language might read: "Once the returned material has been received from the customer it is processed in accordance with Procedure 8.3.0, Control of Nonconforming Material. Omit revision levels—unless you're required to include them by a regulatory body. Otherwise, you'll have to revise one procedure every time reference is made to the other . . . for no other reason than to change a revision letter. You end up defeating the purpose, which is to limit the amount of document revisions you have to contend with.

The additional benefit of referencing related documents is that it fosters the internalization of the system approach to managing the organization. It encourages process owners to think about how their processes are linked to other functions in the company.

Your organization might have to consider the need to translate some documents into a second language. Because this can be labor-intensive, costly, and increase the complexity of documentation management, it's probably better to first investigate more appropriate and equally effective methods of communicating requirements.

Ensure that the content of your requirements conforms to regulatory and customer requirements. If the requirement relates to specific information that's already included in a document of external origin, it's appropriate to make reference to it, just as you would with a related internal document. For example, a shipping procedure might say: "The organization complies with international requirements for the shipment of hazardous chemicals as described in (reference the document or statute)."

Be particularly attentive to the use—or overuse—of the word "all" and comparable modifiers such as "never," "always," "every," and the like. Inappropriate use of this particular group of words can skew meaning, making requirements absurd or impossible to achieve. Ask yourself: "Do we really mean all?"

Sometimes, it's absolutely crucial to conduct a particular activity in a specified sequence. It may be a matter of regulatory compliance that a certain signature always precedes the release of a device for shipment. In those instances, "always" is the appropriate word to use in the procedure.

There are many cases, however, where the risks that are engendered by complying—or failing to comply—with an overly restrictive requirement are less obvious. Using "all" or "never" can so restrict process owners that they can't avoid falling into some breach of a defined requirement.

And auditors don't have the prerogative to decide when the organization really means "never" and when it intends to say, ". . . well, hardly ever." So, be judicious and parsimonious in the use of the word "all."

When all is said and done, writing documents boils down to expressing the requirement correctly, thoroughly, and clearly using the most appropriate medium.

Chapter 6

Managing and Maintaining Documents

Maintaining control of your documentation system is a matter of definition and consistency. We've seen that multiple stakeholders share varying degrees of responsibility for different parts of this process. No one person owns all the information that relates to document and data control. Keeping it all together is a matter of ensuring organizational consensus as to who does what and committing to unswerving and uniform implementation of the practices that have been established.

The other consideration is the actual maintenance of the documents themselves. This runs the gamut from preventing coffee stains on blueprints to backing up the server.

CONTROLLED VS. UNCONTROLLED

We need to begin by establishing what it means for a document to be "controlled":

- The revision status must be known.
- The authorization and approval must be apparent.
- The document must be protected from damage, destruction, or unauthorized revision
- It must be protected from unintended use.

The revision status can be expressed in terms of consecutive letter or number sequences and/or by date. For lengthier documents, some organizations have different revision levels for each of the sections. This is particularly true when they combine all their procedures into one document. Revising by section avoids the need to review the entire document when a small localized change is all that's required.

Revision control serves two functions for users:

- It allows them to differentiate between what the requirement was last month and what it currently is, for example, after the customer has modified the specification.
- It's the single most effective tool for matching requirements that are found on multiple documents. For example, fulfilling an order might involve generating a documentation packet that contains the following:
  - ☐ Customer purchase order
  - ☐ Internal sales order
  - ☐ Production traveler
  - ☐ Inspection form
  - ☐ Drawing
  - ☐ Certificate of compliance

Revision control ensures that the various documents correspond.

Electronic Media

For electronic media, revision can be denoted by last date modified or by saving the file with a new name indicating date or revision.

Approval and authorization generally is denoted through a signature. However, the advent of electronic media has introduced the concept of electronic signatures. This is accomplished through software that provides the necessary security to ensure the information's integrity. Authorization can also be implied. Typical examples might include the following:

- The release of product specifications that can only originate from password-protected files signifies that approval has occurred.
- Purchase orders that are e-mailed to vendors are assumed to be controlled because only the purchasing staff can access the MRP database, and each person has his or her own unique password to access vendors' e-mail addresses.

Protecting documents means ensuring that access is restricted to those who know how to take care of them. For example, electronic media aren't accessible to individuals who could inadvertently alter or corrupt the data. Hard copies of documents must be protected from the elements. Drawings are kept in fireproof cabinets; people who use documents are instructed not to keep food or drink in the same area. Individuals using them are trained not to make notations on the documents unless they are authorized to do so.

Finally, documents contain proprietary information. Customer drawings can contain intellectual property and trade secrets. Care should be taken to ensure that the information isn't accidentally divulged to a competitor—or to anyone else who shouldn't see the information. The best way to ensure the security of this kind of information is to train the process owners in appropriate protocols, like not leaving the documents open on their desks or at their workstations.

An uncontrolled document is one in which any of the characteristics of revision status, approval, and security aren't ensured. Many organizations explicitly state that only electronic versions of documents are considered controlled. Once a document is printed, the hard copy is presumed to be uncontrolled, and the user becomes responsible for verifying the correctness of the information before use.

Paper Documentation

For the many organizations whose documentation system is still predominantly paper, one simple rule usually works: If it isn't signed, it's not controlled. A similar protocol applies to revisions and other changes to documents. The instruction in this case is: If changes are made to a drawing, process sheet, or other specification, they must be initialed and dated by a supervisor or other authorized person.

There's nothing wrong with uncontrolled documents. They can be used provided that they're backed up by a controlled version or the information contained therein is for guidance only and not subject to quality management system (QMS), customer, or regulatory mandates. Helpful tips, memos, and general instructions can be effective without being prescriptive. Explanatory notes penciled into the margins by authorized personnel shouldn't invalidate a document's integrity or usefulness.

It's not necessary to stamp documents "uncontrolled." That practice is needless and cumbersome, often leaving individuals baffled as to the status of anything that doesn't have an uncontrolled stamp.

Training

One of the most effective tools for ensuring document control is training. Often, companies assume that everyone automatically knows about document maintenance and control. Consequently, in the absence of adequate instruction, individuals make their own decisions and do the best they can with what's handed to them. The unfortunate outcome is that, despite the best of intentions, things go awry. Unapproved documents get used; product is built using obsolete drawings; master copies of specifications get discarded. Organizations should take the time to train people in the correct use and care of documents, including access, preservation, and recognizing their status.

More specific training is appropriate depending on the industry. For printed circuit board assembly, for example, it's quite common to have several documents at varying levels. The finished part number has one revision number, while the raw board, bill of materials, and surface mount technology (SMT) files are at different revision levels. In this case, the requirement isn't that all revisions have identical letters; it's for the individuals involved to understand the system of revisions to determine if they have the correct set of documents. In any company that utilizes configuration management, tracking revisions is critical to document control.

CONDITION OF OLD DOCUMENTS

Repeat orders are one of the goals of businesses. Typically, customers place monthly requisitions or annual blanket orders for the same product. And every time the job goes out to the floor, the drawings get pulled and sent out with the document package. Process owners need to assess the condition of documents periodically, especially items like drawings and schematics, to make sure they're still usable. You should consider replacing documents if:

- They're soiled and grimy
- They have food or beverage stains
- The ink has smeared
- The print is faded
- There are so many notes, it's no longer possible to determine which ones are approved
- They're torn at the crease lines from being folded and unfolded hundreds of times

- The edges are shredding beyond the borders and up into the area where specs are found
- They're covered with so much machine-room oil that they're becoming translucent.

For electronic media there are two basic considerations. The first is to protect files with appropriate virus protection software to ensure they don't become corrupted. This often involves acquiring and using software to create firewalls and restrict downloading of unauthorized files from the Internet. Some software programs also contain self-diagnostic features to protect against data corruption. The second maintenance consideration for electronic files involves a periodic backup of the system to ensure continued integrity and access to data in the event of a system crash.

OBSOLETE DOCUMENTS

A document is obsolete if it's no longer correct, has been superseded by a later revision, the product it applies to has been discontinued, or if someone who's authorized decrees it so for any other reason.

Obsolete documents must be retrieved from any area where they could inadvertently be used. They can be discarded or clearly designated as obsolete.

The only time when other actions are appropriate is when you're required to do something else by a customer or a regulatory body. For example, some customers want to retrieve obsolete documents so that they have exclusive control of them. Regulated industries often are required to maintain obsolete documents in an accessible and controlled format for an extended period of time.

The best hedge against having obsolete documents floating around your organization is, again, training. Instruct process owners that it's not OK to keep an obsolete copy of a document in their desks. Let them know that if they ever need it again for any reason, you'll make them another copy.

ACCESS

Appropriate access is a balancing act between ensuring that documents are available to people when they need them and safeguarding against deliberate or unintended misuse. Process owners need to be able to get their hands on all their tools—and that includes the necessary documents. However, overburdening a department or an individual with unnecessary information just creates clutter and increases the likelihood of confusion. The less stuff there is to manage, the better.

The use of electronic media is increasing in popularity because it decreases paperwork and the number of "uncontrolled" documents floating around a facility. There are two factors to consider when assessing appropriate access:

- Is the person authorized to access the document(s)? Authorization is often granted by issuing passwords. If you have the password, you have access.
- Does the person know how to find the document(s)? It's not uncommon that people have access to documents but are unable to navigate the organization's electronic infrastructure. Should something happen to the icon on their desktop, for instance, they're at a lost to find their procedures. If individuals have no idea how to find their documents on the server, it's tantamount to not having access.

A variation on these same factors applies to hard copies of specifications and requirements. If the procedures and work instructions are kept in a binder, do the process owners know where the binder is stored? Should a person have access to certain documents? And does that person know how to use the information and protect it? If the answer is "no," then the organization needs to exercise appropriate control to restrict access.

DOCUMENTS OF EXTERNAL ORIGIN

Control of documents of external origin doesn't differ significantly from internal documentation. You must know the revision level, that the document is authorized, and how to preserve it and keep it secure.

If the documents belong to your customer, control means making sure you have the correct revision and that the proprietary information is secure. Your document control procedure should say how you do that, especially if you handle security differently than you would with your own documents.

Repair manuals and user guides generally don't change unless you purchase an upgrade. Control of these documents is limited to appropriate storage and access.

Figure 6.1	Matrix of Documents of External Origin	

Document	Location	Responsible department or individual
ISO 9000 or ANSI quality standards	Quality assurance department	QA manager
Customer drawings or specifications	Sales office	Customer service manager
UL documents and requirements	Engineering office	Director of engineering
Maintenance manuals	PM manager's office	Supervisor of equipment maintenance

Industrial and regulatory requirements and standards are similarly controlled. An added consideration with things like military specifications is that the organization might not have all the documents at its facility. Rather, control is exercised by being able to access and/or acquire the correct version via a Web site or through some other form of communication. The challenge is to ensure that individuals consistently follow protocols for contacting issuing organizations to ensure that specifications haven't changed.

The most efficient way to ensure adequate control of documents of external origin is to create a matrix that identifies ownership and location. The rest of the details can be left to the individual process owners, provided an assessment or internal audit reveals that the control each owner exercises is adequate. If the control is closely linked to similar internal documents—for example, production drawings—it may be important to ensure that the interrelation is defined in your document control procedure.

The matrix of documents of external origin might look like the one in Figure 6.1.

TIPS FOR MANAGING DOCUMENTATION

Managing all your documents and the many different considerations they engender is actually a subset of managing your entire QMS. If you understand and can define the interrelations, you have a good grasp of how the entire system works.

The manner in which you manage documentation is a process—just like any other in your QMS. The document control system can't be arbitrarily deployed or sporadically adhered to. You must identify responsibilities, describe activities, define inputs and outputs, allocate adequate resources, ensure uniform implementation, and generate appropriate records.

Establishing your QMS documentation system is dependent on how well you define the various features of this process. Once you have defined the activities, their sequence, and interactions, you can create the document control procedure that you'll use to define and control the requirements of the entire process.

There's no single prescribed "best way" for managing your documentation. As you can see from the preceding chapters, there are hundreds of combinations and permutations of documents, owners, practices, and methods of control.

However, here are a few suggestions to help you out:

- *Study other processes to see how they individually handle documents.* Don't be afraid to ask people questions. What does engineering do when it receives electronic data from a customer? Who looks at the attached customer orders and specifications when an order comes in? How does the manufacturing supervisor assemble the document package to build a device? Who schedules the field service installations? How does information about customer complaints make it to the customer contact database? Who has access to the information, and how is it used?

  Managing these interfaces is a large part of managing your documents because each document is the articulation of a requirement that must be fulfilled, usually through another process, like inspection, purchasing, or design.

- *Once you have a handle on the interfaces, you must manage your documents within those constraints.* If you find gaps, facilitate filling them. For example, ISO 9001:2000 has a requirement in 7.2.1 relative to ensuring that appropriate consideration is given to any regulatory or statutory requirements. You can help to bring consistency to the fulfillment of this requirement by establishing a protocol that describes where the regulations are located, how they're accessed, and what record must be created signifying that the review of statutory requirements has occurred.

- *A review of documentation practices might yield the discovery that duplication is increasing the risk of confusion and error.* You can streamline the process by eliminating redundancy and increasing efficiency and reliability.

- *Get everyone on board.* Conduct training. Share ownership.

■ *Recognize that smaller systems exist within your larger document control.* They don't all have to be the same, but they do have to function together as a system. CAD files are maintained differently from production routers. They're controlled by functions in departments peopled by individuals with different expertise, skills, and responsibilities. But at some defined juncture, they must converge and mesh.

■ *Make sure you have adequate resources—and that includes both time and people.* Document control isn't an occasional activity when we have time. It's an integral part of making sure your entire QMS works. Calculate the time and whatever other costs, and make sure top management understands the need to allocate adequate resources.

■ *Software packages for managing your documentation abound.* They facilitate interfaces between databases, such as customer complaints and corrective actions. They handle security, interpret or manipulate data, and facilitate information analysis. They make possible electronic approvals and myriad hyperlinks between created documents using different software packages. If you decide to use one of the many products on the market, assess its applicability to your own organization. Consider:

☐ Complexity of the software package
☐ Plug-in modules
☐ Compatibility to existing electronic infrastructure
☐ Relevance of some of the features to your own organization
☐ Sophistication of your own staff
☐ Longevity
☐ Return on investment

If personnel outside the information management system department purchase new software programs or introduce new data into the system, they need to communicate with IMS staff to ensure that the software is compatible.

This is your documentation system. It must work for you. How you manage and control it is your responsibility and your prerogative.

Chapter 7

Handling Revisions and Deviations

One of the distinguishing attributes of a well-implemented quality management system (QMS) is its dynamic nature. Things change; that's a fundamental and critical feature of your QMS. If they don't change, they can't improve. ISO 9004:2000 lists continual improvement as one of the eight quality management principles. There's a direct correlation between the way an organization handles change and the resulting improvements.

ISO 9001:2000 specifically addresses change in subclause 5.4.2 b: ". . . the integrity of the quality management system is maintained when changes to the quality management system are planned and implemented." Because part of the system's integrity is vested in the manner in which you define and control requirements, it follows that the tools that you use—i.e., documents—must exhibit a comparable reliability. The integrity of your documentation must remain constant in the midst of change.

With few exceptions, organizations don't halt all activity when it becomes apparent that either a process or a requirement must be amended. Manufacturing has to continue; services must be provided; customers' orders need to be filled. The challenge is ensuring that documents are current and relevant, even as you revise them so they conform to changing requirements. It can easily become a chicken-or-the-egg conundrum, where you can't decide whether to change the document first or the practice the document defines. You can't avoid acting on this because things are always changing. Schedules get updated, designs get improved, customers change the order quantity, a new piece of equipment comes in, you find a new vendor, or the ISO standard gets revised. So how do you control documents when they're undergoing revision?

A multitude of methods exist for doing this, but regardless of the method, there's one governing rule: communication. The second and almost as important rule is:

record the communication. You can be forgiven just about any breach that comes under the nonconformance umbrella of "not conducting process in accordance with documented procedure" if you've told someone that the procedure is being revised—and you have evidence to prove it.

This doesn't absolve organizations from their responsibility of maintaining the level of document control that's prescribed in certain industries. Rules governing key processes can't be ignored. Constraints applied in regulated industries protect an organization from a figurative QMS meltdown or your customer from harm. Comments and tips made in this chapter relative to notations on specifications or the use of temporary documents are made with the express proviso that they apply *only in those instances where the practice is allowed by the regulatory agency or other governing body.*

REVIEW AND APPROVAL PROCESS

It is OK to write on a document, provided you say it's OK and you establish the appropriate criteria. For example, does your document control procedure identify who's authorized to annotate a document and under what conditions the practice is acceptable?

There are several circumstances that warrant the use of accepted practices for making notations on documents.

- *Procedure and/or process has changed.* One of the most efficient methods for ensuring control when things are in the middle of changes is to have what's referred to as a "red line" document. The authorized process owner analyzes the current document against existing or new practices, determines the necessary changes, marks up the current revision of the procedure or work instruction with red ink (or any color, as long as it's noticeable), and signs and dates the document. The established practice is to allow others to use the document for a predetermined time period or until the approved master is signed off. This method can save time and needless bureaucratic steps. Once a new revision is approved, the marked-up document is retained to provide an accurate history of the nature of the changes that were made.
- *Specification has changed, but the customer hasn't sent in a revised drawing.* Again, it's perfectly acceptable to use a drawing that has notes that have been dated and signed. These will relate to changes in dimension, mate-

rial, assembly, or some other attribute. The stipulation with notations on prints is that users must be able to differentiate the notes that relate to requirements from those that have been added to explain the process.

For example, there might be two notes on a print for a wire assembly. The first indicates that the customer has revised the product so that it's one inch longer. This is a customer-specified requirement. The second note has been added by the group leader reminding the assembler how far back to strip the wires to get a good crimp. This one is a guidance note and is used to facilitate the process to help the assembler fulfill the requirement. Although it's probably a good idea to have both notes signed and dated, it's also important to recognize which notes are part of the product requirement and which are more in the nature of helpful hints.

Variations on the cases mentioned could include:

☐ Schedule changes

☐ Customer change orders

☐ Adjustments to machine profiles and/or settings

☐ One-time concessions

In each case, the person authorized to make the changes should be identified in your procedure. The production supervisor may be the only person who can change the schedule; the purchasing agent can sign-off on a concession on an incoming order. Authorized notations on documents are an acceptable method for dealing with change, provided the practice itself is tightly controlled and uniformly implemented.

When a document is in the process of being revised, it's important to communicate its status to process owners. If the documents are hard copy, they should be marked or appended with an authorized note stating that the document is being changed, and guidance or approval must be sought before use. The process owner then knows to ask a supervisor before using the document. In small organizations, a brief note should suffice. However, in larger organizations with more procedures to contend with, a more formal process is warranted.

For procedure and work instructions, controlling and communicating in-process revisions in a process can be accomplished using the master document list. These are often maintained in a spreadsheet or Microsoft Word table. Simply add a column headed "Status" and indicate when a document is in revision. Highlighting helps to make it more noticeable.

In some organizations the review and approval process is more elaborate and requires multiple signatories, including some external authorizations. The progress made toward releasing the new revision can be compared to the method you'd use to track the status of a product that's being manufactured. In those instances, the method of recording and communicating the status of a document undergoing revision is itself a kind of documentation that must be controlled.

DEVIATIONS

Deviation notices are one of the most efficient tools for handling temporary documentation changes (see Figure 7.1). A deviation notice is a document that allows the use of an alternate method, process, component, or supplier. It's usually used for a predetermined time or until, for example, a machine can be fixed, a problem is solved, or inventory is replenished. Generally, the deviation doesn't affect the product or change the output of the process. Basically it says, "This authorizes the user to deviate from the documented procedure or specification in this defined manner: . . ." It will reference the related documents such as the procedure, work instruction, drawing, bill of material, form, or other specification.

This reinforces the concept that even in the midst of change, it's important to maintain control. It also provides the necessary evidence that the individuals had the appropriate authorization for the action they took.

A typical scenario might involve an out-of-stock component. The alternate source for the component hasn't been approved yet, but they have the parts you need to complete your customer's order. You initiate a deviation notice to allow the use of the alternate supplier and to signal a change on the bill of materials, despite the fact that the new company hasn't yet been added to your approved vendor list. Another case might involve outsourcing a process that's generally done in-house. Or it could involve a change to the sequence of processes to accommodate a bottleneck or deal with the suspected root cause of a problem.

The important thing to remember with deviation notices is that they must be monitored. The problem that often arises is that, although they're initiated to authorize and control a deviation to a defined requirement as a temporary solution, individuals aren't as diligent about closing them out when they expire—or in updating them if they need to be continued beyond the originally anticipated timeframe. It often happens that the temporary deviation becomes the regular practice, and no one updates the accompanying documents. Or, if the organiza-

Figure 7.1	Deviation Notice

(This form is used as a temporary authorization to deviate from a documented procedure or specification.)

Date: _____   **Requested by:** _____

Effective dates: beginning ____/____/____   **until** ____/____/____
* If duration is unknown, explain below
Initiate corrective or preventive action?   ☐ **Yes**   ☐ **No**

Nature of deviation:

☐ Raw material substitution   ☐ Process change
☐ Component substitution   ☐ Alternate supplier
☐ Use of alternate equipment   ☐ Other

(Briefly describe the nature of the deviation and the reason.)

Authorized by: (A minimum of two signatures is required, including manager's or process owner's of the affected product or process.)

President _____
Operations manager _____
Purchasing director _____
Director of sales/customer service _____
Document control manager _____
Quality engineer _____

Date deviation discontinued: ____/____/____   **Closed out by:** _____

tion has a large turnover in personnel and the deviation was prolonged, you could end up with two groups of people conducting the same process using different tools, materials, or methods. The potential for error, or at least inconsistency, is substantial.

When deviation notices are tightly monitored and controlled, they're a simple and efficient tool for handling temporary changes. The only drawback to their use arises when process owners fail to follow through and close them out.

ENGINEERING CHANGE NOTICES

An engineering change notice (ECN) is the tool used to control revisions to products, processes, and documents. It differs from deviation notices in that the resulting actions are permanent. The engineering change notice serves to alert process owners that a change is coming.

ECNs vary extensively in their use. There are many different styles of forms and electronic programs for generating them, accommodating the great variety of industries and users. They might simply serve to communicate an impending revision, or they can be the instruments for controlling an entire process. In its simplest form, an ECN describes the change and provides evidence of authorization. Depending on an organization's complexity, it might also launch a review to verify the continued applicability and conformity of related documents, procedures, and specifications. It might entail multiple reviews and several authorizing signatures.

In some organizations, the ECN is the only document used to define the change to the specification. Although uncommon, it's an accepted practice in some industries to have product documentation packets with ECNs describing requirements that supersede previous revisions. Rather than generate new specifications, the engineering staff simply generates an ECN referencing the changes. This can save a great deal of time and resources, especially if creating new production drawings would necessitate transferring guidance notes, color coding, and other production information.

Some organizations use ECNs for all document changes, thereby ensuring that the specification's status is controlled during the revision process.

Engineering change notices may be too time-consuming for smaller organizations. However, for large companies, they're one of the most reliable methods for ensuring the integrity of documented requirements when things change.

FAILURE MODES AND EFFECTS ANALYSIS (FMEA)

FMEA is used to identify and analyze potential problems, either with products or processes, for the purpose of prevention. Most people think of an FMEA as a one-time event that becomes a record encompassing a prioritized list of risks for the purpose of future decision making.

In fact, a good FMEA is a living document that's continually revised as potential problems are addressed. It establishes the justification for changes to existing products and facilitates the definition of requirements and specification for new designs as well as their related processes. No action is without consequence, and the FMEA is periodically revised to assess the risks engendered by changes that have been implemented. As such, the FMEA is a great vehicle for orchestrating document changes. FMEA is about managing the risk from potential problems; document control is about managing the tools you use to define the requirements that are the subject of the FMEA.

FMEA allows an organization to be proactive in revisions to designs, processes, and attending documents by anticipating the requisite changes before problems arise. It encourages organizations to think systemwide when they make decisions so they can perceive the effects those changes can have on other functions, including documentation.

DESIGN PLANS

Design plans are included in this list because they include, as their input, specifications. Those specifications might relate to form, fit, and function. They might also relate to packaging, labeling, user manuals, software, regulatory mandates, validation criteria, or a host of other requirements. Keeping a tight rein on the definition of these inputs involves document control. There's perhaps no part of the organization where change is more expected and likely. Things change a lot when you're designing a product. If they didn't, the new product offerings would probably not be very exciting.

How do you control those changes to the design specifications? How do you ensure that the final output of the process is what was required, especially if there have been numerous changes? How do you ensure that the manufacturing drawings and purchasing specifications have remained current in this bubbling cauldron of ideas that ultimately will produce the recipe for your company's next big thing?

Failure to adequately control the documentation related to product design can, and often does, result in miscommunications that delay release and cause needless problems when the product is finally delivered to the customer.

Make sure that your design process adequately defines the method of controlling the mass of documents that will be generated. Decide how the changes to specifications will be communicated and determine what kinds of changes will involve interfaces with other departments and functions. Otherwise, you can expect to generate a lot of engineering change notices after the product is released.

In all cases, you must ensure that changes to documents are recorded. For procedures, this is often done by creating a "revision history" section at the end of each. Typically, it has the date of each revision, revision level (e.g., A, B, C, etc.), and a description of the changes that were made. For electronic files, the older revisions are often archived in a separate file with limited access. Hard copy documents can be similarly archived. Instead of having an actual summary, the reader is required to compare each document to find the changes. In most cases, this isn't particularly arduous and saves the time of generating a report about the changes. The nature of the documents and the kinds of revisions will drive decisions regarding appropriate traceability. Common sense should prevail.

A common thread runs through this chapter: In all instances, good document-revision control is characterized by effective communication, consistent practices, and reliable record retention. Have an established method for letting people know when documents are changing. Make sure people have the right information, despite the changes, so you can continue to serve your customers. Instill a commitment to consistency. It's important for everyone to comprehend equally the importance of complying with the process you develop for handling changes to documents. Always keep records of what has been changed and who authorized it.

Chapter 8

Writing Document Control Procedures

I t's important that you write your procedure for document and data control *after* you've figured out what documentation you have. That's why this chapter falls at the end of the book. You can't describe your process until you have an idea what your process (or processes) look like. Otherwise it would be like writing a manufacturing specification for a device you haven't yet designed. Therefore, assess what kind of documents you have, how many different "owners" share responsibility, how many different kinds of media you employ to communicate requirements, and how much control is appropriate for your organization.

Document control procedures are similar to others used to describe quality management system (QMS) processes such as internal auditing and corrective action because they're often presumed to be generic. After all, how much possible difference could there be in the way organizations handle their documents? Because of this presumption, it's not uncommon for companies to purchase boilerplate procedures purporting to comply with a requisite QMS standard. These procedures might help ensure that you cover all the requirements your registrar or certifying body mandates. They might also serve as a skeletal foundation for defining your process. But they don't say what your organization does. Like all your other documents, this procedure must be helpful to your process owners or it's a waste of time. It has to describe what you do.

FOCUS ON THE INTENDED AUDIENCE

Consider this procedure in the same light as a work instruction. People will refer to this document for information about document control. This is where they'll go to find out:

- How to access the documents they need

- Who's authorized to approve or revise a document
- What they should do if they think a document is wrong
- How to write a document
- The definitions for deviation notices and engineering change notices
- How they can tell if their document is the latest revision
- What "controlled" means
- What to do with old or obsolete documents

The other thing to remember is that the entire organization is your audience because everyone uses one kind of document or another every day. Moreover, the procedure must convey the fact that this document isn't just about quality procedures but about all the organization's documents—including CAD files and manuals and contracts and your Web site.

For larger organizations you may wish to have a document and data control procedure that describes general practices and supplemental work instructions, or comparable documents that define specific tasks and protocols. For example, it would be appropriate to reference existing documented protocols for backing up electronic media or preserving hard copy blueprints. Depending on your industry, you might also create a defined process for handling customers' drawings, electronic media, and other intellectual properties. As with other processes, it's a good practice to utilize the well-defined documents that already exist. They usually provide the best description for the process in a format that's most comprehensible to the user.

Take a look at the extensive array of documents in Chapter 2 and identify those that apply to your organization. This will help you define the scope of your procedure. It will also help you to identify the various process owners and individuals who are authorized to access, approve, create, review, or amend specific kinds of documents.

ENLIST PROCESS OWNERS

Identifying process owners will provide you with a list of individuals you'll need to interview. Unless you're planning on owning every single, solitary, blessed document in your organization, this is the time to start sharing. Ask the engineering staff to describe how they control their documents. Find out if they have their own written guidelines and procedures. (You'll be surprised how many of them do.) Explain to them that this information must be included in the procedure because their documents are part of the documentation infrastructure. Do the same with the customer service department, production supervisors, purchasing agents, technical support, or any other function that has ownership of documents.

Create a chart like the one in Figure 8.1. It will help you sort things out as you develop your procedure. You can use the chart as a guide to organize information

Figure 8.1 Sample Chart of Documents and Authorized Individuals

Function	Document	Individual	Authorization/Responsibility
Purchasing	Purchase order	Purchasing agent	Place any < $100,000; approve changes including cancellations
		President/general manager	Countersign orders > $100,000
	Approved vendor list	Purchasing agent	Additions, deletions, changes in status
Production	Traveler/router	Operations manager	Approve; amend
		Production supervisor	Amend
		Manufacturing engineer	Create; approve; amend
		Machine operators	Access; read- or print-only
	Production schedule	Scheduler	Create; amend
		Operations manager	Approve; amend
		Production supervisor	Amend
Customer service	Quotations	Customer service manager	Create; approve; amend
		Customer service representative	Create; approve < $5,000
		Order entry	Access; read-only
	Customer complaint database	Customer service manager	Access, update, create reports, link to other databases
		Sales manager	Access; read-only
		Customer service representative	Limited access, data entry, read-only, no post-entry amendments
		Information management director	Access; maintain electronic infrastructure

and outline your procedure. It will also help you keep track of the people you've interviewed so that you don't forget anyone. Or you can formalize the chart and use it as an addendum to your procedure. Personally, I like charts because they provide a handy reference. Their drawback is that keeping the information current can become cumbersome. Putting them in an addendum, however, allows you to revise the chart without having to revise the entire procedure.

Talk to the process owners. Find out what kinds of documents they use, where they get them from, how they're stored, and what happens when they must be revised. When interviewing them steer clear of "quality" words like "document" and "procedure." The toolmaker uses drawings; the purchasing manager, the MRP database; the service tech, schematics and test software.

Let the information technology people write the section on electronic media. They have answers to questions you haven't even thought up yet. They in turn could benefit from a documented procedure that defines things like:

- Who's authorized to introduce new software programs into the system
- The rules governing creating new files and folders on the server
- Rules on how to name files to ensure consistency
- Who's authorized to create and update hyperlinks
- Whom to talk to for different problems
- What information should be on the server rather than on personal computers
- And always: access, access, access

WRITING WITH ISO 9001:2000 IN MIND

Once you've gathered the information you need, you can write the procedure. Figure 8.2 shows the requirements for a documented procedure relating to the control of documents as found in subclause 4.2.3 of ISO 9001:2000. Remember that these requirements apply to all the documents you use to fulfill customer requirements and manage your QMS.

a) ". . . approve documents for adequacy prior to use"
- For each category of documents, who are the individuals who determine if they're adequate and approve them for use?
- Is more than one approval required?
- Do you have electronic signature approval?

Figure 8.2	Requirements for a Documented Procedure

"A documented procedure shall be established to define the controls needed:

a) To approve documents prior to issue

b) To review and update as necessary and re-approve documents

c) To ensure that changes and the current revision status of documents are identified

d) To ensure that relevant versions of applicable documents are available at point of use

e) To ensure that documents remain legible and readily identifiable

f) To ensure that documents of external origin are identified and their distribution controlled

g) To prevent the unintended use of obsolete documents, and to apply documentation to them if they are retained for any purpose."

---

b) ". . . review and update . . . and re-approve . . . "
- How and under what circumstances are documents reviewed and updated?
- Who's responsible for the review? For the re-approval?

c) ". . . changes and the current revision status are identified"
- How do you denote revision? By date? By number or letter?
- How about revisions to electronic documents such CAD files?
- What's the process for indicating the version of software that's loaded into a device if you have more than one version?
- Where do you keep the record of changes, at the end of the document or in a separate file?

d) ". . . relevant versions of applicable documents are available at point of use"
- How do people access the documents they need? Electronic or hard copy?

■ Do individuals know where to find the documents they need on the server?

■ Who's responsible for distribution?

e) ". . . documents remain legible and readily identifiable"

■ Are prints worn, torn, or faded? Who checks this?

■ How identifiable are the names of electronic files?

■ Are handwritten notes decipherable?

f) ". . . documents of external origin are identified and their distribution controlled"

■ Do you know what external documents the organization uses?

■ Is someone responsible for ensuring their accessibility?

■ How do you know if the documents have been superseded?

■ Where are they located?

g) ". . . prevent the unintended use of obsolete documents, and to apply suitable identification to them if they are retained . . ."

■ Who's responsible for retrieving obsolete documents?

■ Who removes or restricts access to obsolete electronic documents?

■ How do you indicate obsolete documents that must be kept?

■ Does everyone know how to identify an obsolete document?

Your organization might have additional requirements imposed on it by customers or regulatory bodies. That information should also be included in your procedure.

When writing the procedure, remember the tips from Chapter 5:

■ Be clear and concise

■ Remember your audience and refrain from using jargon

■ Try not to repeat things

■ Refer to other documents when possible or practical

■ Be careful how you use the word "all."

Appendix

This appendix contains sample forms for:
- Document/corresponding record chart
- Matrix of documents of external origin
- Deviation notice
- Sample worksheet for documents and authorized individuals

Document/Corresponding Record Chart

Document	Requirement	Record	Alternate evidence of fulfillment

Matrix of Documents of External Origin

Document	Location	Responsible Department or Individual

Deviation Notice

(This form is used as a temporary authorization to deviate from a documented procedure or specification.)

Date: _____   **Requested by:** _____

Effective dates: beginning ____/____/____   **until** ____/____/____
* If duration is unknown, explain below
Initiate corrective or preventive action?   ☐ **Yes**   ☐ **No**

Nature of deviation:

☐ Raw material substitution   ☐ Process change
☐ Component substitution   ☐ Alternate supplier
☐ Use of alternate equipment   ☐ Other

(Briefly describe the nature of the deviation and the reason.)

Authorized by: (A minimum of two signatures is required, including manager's or process owner's of the affected product or process.)

President _____
Operations manager _____
Purchasing director _____
Director of sales/customer service _____
Document control manager _____
Quality engineer _____

Date deviation discontinued: ____/____/____   **Closed out by:** _____

Sample Worksheet for Documents and Authorized Individuals

Function	Document	Individual	Authorization/Responsibility